I0012313

MRBEAST UNAUTHORIZED BIO

The Inspiring Journey of MrBeast From Viral Videos to Global Impact

DOORS JOHNS

TABLE OF CONTENT

CHAPTER 1: THE BIRTH OF A VISIONARY

1.1 Early Life and Inspirations

Jimmy Donaldson, known to the world as MrBeast, was born on May 7, 1998, in Greenville, North Carolina. From an early age, he exhibited a distinct curiosity and ingenuity that marked him apart. Growing up in a humble environment, Jimmy spent most of his youth exploring his hobbies, which varied from video games to storytelling. These early years were essential in forming his view on life and his future objectives.

Jimmy's upbringing was distinguished by a preoccupation with technology. He was the sort of child who would spend hours playing with his computer, not just to play games but to learn how things functioned. This interest expanded to the internet, where he found a limitless universe of possibilities. His passion for video games brought him to sites like YouTube, where players shared their experiences, advice, and successes. These films kindled a flame in him, prompting him to dream of one day making his own material.

Another big effect on young Jimmy was his family. While not affluent, his family stressed the significance of hard work, compassion, and persistence. These beliefs constituted the cornerstone of his personality and subsequently played a significant part in creating his distinctive approach to content development. Watching his mother's passion and perseverance taught him the significance of persistence, a virtue that would become important in his YouTube adventure.

At school, Jimmy was not very academically oriented. He frequently thought that the standard schooling system did not accommodate to his artistic tendencies. Despite this, he excelled in areas that needed problem-solving and ingenuity. He was the sort of kid who would come up with unique answers to difficulties, frequently surprise his professors and classmates. This capacity to think beyond the box became one of his greatest assets.

Books and movies also had a part in developing Jimmy's viewpoint. Stories of heroes overcoming challenges and making a difference resonated profoundly with him. He was especially moved by storylines that stressed the necessity of giving back and helping others. These anecdotes created the roots of compassion and altruism that would ultimately characterize his reputation.

1.2 Discovering YouTube

Jimmy's adventure into the world of YouTube started in 2012 when he was only 13 years old. The platform was still in its nascent years, but it had already begun to transform how consumers received information. Jimmy was attracted by the concept of regular folks generating content and developing communities around their hobbies. To him, YouTube was more than simply a website; it was a canvas for creation.

Inspired by creators who offered gaming material, tutorials, and comedy routines, Jimmy decided to establish his own channel. At start, it was a small undertaking. Armed with a rudimentary microphone and an ancient computer, he started posting films under the pseudonym "MrBeast6000." His early output was a combination of gaming videos, commentary, and experimentation with new forms. Like many novices, his earliest movies were far from professional, but they displayed his passion to learn and develop.

One of the issues Jimmy had during this era was matching his newfound enthusiasm with school and family commitments. His mother, although sympathetic, was anxious about his academic performance. She encouraged him to concentrate on his education, but Jimmy was certain that YouTube held the key to his future. Despite their periodic conflicts, Jimmy's mother had a significant part in supporting his aspirations, even if she didn't completely comprehend them at the time.

Jimmy's early videos failed to acquire attention. He sometimes felt irritated by the lack of opinions and interaction, but he refused to quit up. Instead, he committed himself to learning the platform. He spent many hours examining successful artists, learning about video titles, thumbnails, and viewer behavior. This era of trial and error was important in helping him comprehend the complexities of YouTube's algorithm.

As he continued to submit movies, Jimmy started to get a deeper grasp of his skills. He discovered that his love for experimenting and his readiness to take chances set him different. Whether it was tackling uncommon gaming challenges or producing innovative content ideas, Jimmy's channel began to draw a tiny but dedicated following. These early backers supplied the encouragement he needed to keep going.

1.3 The First Steps: MrBeast6000

The moniker "MrBeast6000" may sound strange, but it showed Jimmy's young inventiveness and drive. He adopted the moniker without much consideration, but it rapidly became associated with his online image. Under this guise, Jimmy went on a quest that would ultimately make him one of the most known people on the internet.

In the early days of MrBeast6000, the material was diverse and experimental. Jimmy tried his hand at everything from Minecraft gaming to funny comments on viral videos. While these films were far from the high-production extravaganza he's renowned for today, they highlighted his tireless passion to create and share.

One of Jimmy's first important successes came with a series of films centered on gaming problems. For instance, he generated material around games like "Call of Duty" and "Minecraft," where he would establish unique goals and chronicle his efforts to attain them. These videos connected with gamers who respected his humor and dedication. Slowly but surely, his subscription count started to increase.

Another turning point occurred when Jimmy began to concentrate on making "oddly satisfying" material. He discovered that some sorts of films, such as time-lapse footage or compilation movies, did well on the site. By putting his own perspective on these trends, he managed to reach a bigger audience. His ability to detect and capitalize on emerging trends became one of his distinguishing attributes.

Despite his burgeoning success, Jimmy stayed grounded. He continued to communicate with his audience, regularly reacting to comments and soliciting recommendations for future films. This level of involvement helped him develop a solid community around his channel. He knew that YouTube was not only about providing content but also about engaging with people.

As the years went by, Jimmy's material developed. He proceeded to invest on better equipment and started cooperating with other producers. These partnerships helped him to reach new audiences and learn from his colleagues. Each step pushed him closer to reaching his aim of being a full-time content maker.

The trip of MrBeast6000 was not without its hurdles. Jimmy encountered times of self-doubt and criticism from individuals who didn't comprehend his objectives. However, he remained persistent in his notion that YouTube was his calling. This constant commitment, paired with his readiness to adapt and innovate, created the ground for his stratospheric ascension.

The narrative of MrBeast's early years is a monument to the power of enthusiasm, tenacity, and ingenuity. From an inquisitive boy in Greenville to a burgeoning multimedia maker, Jimmy Donaldson's adventure was just starting. Little did he realize, the lessons he learnt during these formative years would build the groundwork for a profession that would impact not just his life but also the lives of millions throughout the globe.

.

CHAPTER 2: THE RISE TO STARDOM

2.1 Viral Videos and Breakthrough Moments

Jimmy Donaldson—better known as MrBeast— did not earn celebrity overnight. His journey to popularity was a mix of persistent work, inventive innovation, and the odd stroke of luck. The path to viral stardom started with his first important breakthrough video, one that would serve as a pattern for his future success.

One of MrBeast's initial popular videos was his ambitious endeavor to count to 100,000 on camera. This initiative, which required him to sit for hours and count aloud, was a tribute to his unusual approach to content production. While others pursued trends or mimicked successful producers, Jimmy carved himself a niche by doing something insanely simple but compelling. The video gained millions of views and highlighted his determination to push the bounds of endurance and inventiveness.

This breakthrough constituted a turning point. MrBeast understood that audiences were driven to spectacles, challenges, and material that broke established rules. He started to develop concepts that were not only amusing but also gigantic in magnitude. From trying to remain underwater for 24 hours to watching paint dry for hours on end, Jimmy's movies appealed into viewers' interest and kept them captivated. Each viral moment contributed to his rising image as an innovator on the network.

Another big milestone occurred when MrBeast began giving away enormous amounts of money in his videos. Initially sponsored by sponsorships and his own money, these freebies set him apart from other entrepreneurs. Videos like "Giving $10,000 to a Homeless Man" and "Donating $100,000 to Random People" connected emotionally with viewers. The charity demonstrated in these movies was both refreshing and encouraging, garnering MrBeast a dedicated following and a reputation for philanthropy.

These viral moments were not just about the statistics; they were about the story behind them. Each film presented a message of endurance, generosity, or pure tenacity, which resonated with viewers on a deeper level. MrBeast's ability to mix show with content was a major aspect in his journey to prominence.

2.2 The Power of Consistency

While viral videos were important in catapulting MrBeast to popularity, they were just half of the issue. Consistency was the glue that kept his accomplishments together. Early on, Jimmy knew that to develop a sustainable career on YouTube, he needed to provide high-quality video frequently. This entailed not just posting constantly but also ensuring that each video was better than the previous.

Consistency became a characteristic of MrBeast's channel. He followed to a rigid schedule, investing many hours to preparing, recording, and editing his films. This discipline enabled him to maintain a consistent stream of information that kept his audience interested. Moreover, his devotion to quality guaranteed that viewers knew they could always anticipate something remarkable from his station.

One of the problems of keeping consistency was the ongoing need for new ideas. Unlike producers who could depend on a single format or specialty, MrBeast's brand was founded on inventiveness. This meant that every film had to be larger, better, or more unusual than the previous. To do this, Jimmy surrounded himself with a team of like-minded people who shared his goal. Together, they conceived, planned, and executed some of the most ambitious initiatives on the platform.

Another component of constancy was MrBeast's effort to knowing his audience. He meticulously analyzed statistics, paying attention to what connected with viewers and what didn't. This data-driven strategy enabled him to tweak his material and guarantee that each video was targeted to his audience's tastes. By continually offering value, he was able to create trust and loyalty among his audience.

Consistency also extended to his contacts with supporters. MrBeast makes it a point to communicate with his fanbase via social media, comments, and even physical appearances. This degree of accessibility made him more approachable and developed a feeling of community around his channel. Fans felt that they were part of his journey, which enhanced their attachment to his work.

2.3 Building a Loyal Audience

One of MrBeast's biggest triumphs has been his ability to develop a passionately dedicated fanbase. While many producers struggle to maintain viewers in a competitive digital market, Jimmy has managed to develop a community that not only watches his videos but actively supports his attempts.

The root of this allegiance lays in MrBeast's honesty. From the outset, he has been shamelessly himself, sharing his eccentricities, insecurities, and obsessions with his audience. This honesty has made him sympathetic, even as his celebrity and money have increased. Viewers view him as a real person rather than simply a content generator, which has generated a profound feeling of trust.

Another key in fostering loyalty has been MrBeast's dedication to give back. His humanitarian activities have connected emotionally with viewers, who respect his generosity and desire to utilize his platform for good. Whether it's planting trees with the Team Trees program or cleaning up seas with Team Seas, MrBeast's philanthropic endeavors have encouraged millions to donate to vital causes.

MrBeast has also built loyalty by establishing a feeling of exclusivity and belonging. Through challenges, freebies, and interactive material, he has made his viewers feel like active participants in his quest. For example, his "last to leave" competitions urge followers to compete for life-changing rewards, generating a feeling of excitement and involvement. These participation features have deepened the link between MrBeast and his audience.

Furthermore, MrBeast's capacity to adapt and change has kept his fans committed. He has continuously pushed the frontiers of what's possible on YouTube, whether via larger-than-life pranks, creative formats, or pioneering partnerships. This willingness to take chances and accept change has guaranteed that his work stays new and engaging, keeping people coming back for more.

The commitment of MrBeast's fanbase is arguably best shown by the popularity of his goods and brand expansions. From Beast Burger to his apparel brand, people have welcomed his initiatives with excitement. This degree of support is a monument to the trust and affection he has garnered over the years.

The climb to success for MrBeast was not an instant phenomenon but a product of smart planning, hard work, and an uncompromising devotion to his craft. Through viral videos, constant work, and the development of a dedicated fanbase, Jimmy Donaldson turned himself from a small-town inventor into one of the most prominent characters on the internet.

His path serves as a compelling reminder that with passion, tenacity, and a willingness to take risks, anything is possible.

CHAPTER 3: MASTERING THE ART OF CONTENT CREATION

3.1 Crafting the Perfect Viral Video

The cornerstone of MrBeast's success resides in his extraordinary ability to produce viral material. Crafting a great viral video is both an art and a science, involving a combination of creativity, strategy, and technical knowledge. For Jimmy Donaldson, every video starts with a simple but captivating premise. The main notion is meant to capture attention immediately—whether it's giving away thousands of dollars, enduring severe circumstances, or arranging enormous social experiments.

The first step in developing a viral video is analyzing the audience. MrBeast's crew spends hours examining trends, evaluating metrics, and generating themes that engage with visitors. This audience-first strategy guarantees that each video is relevant, enjoyable, and worth sharing. Additionally, the initial few seconds of the video are essential. MrBeast employs appealing thumbnails, fascinating titles, and high-energy starts to captivate viewers straight away.

Production quality is another key factor. Over the years, MrBeast has spent extensively in equipment, editing tools, and a competent crew to guarantee his movies match the greatest standards. Dynamic imagery, fast-paced editing, and intriguing storyline keep people captivated to the screen. The timing of his films is painstakingly arranged to retain attention and eliminate any uninteresting times.

Another essential factor is the emotional connection. Whether it's the delight of a random act of kindness or the tension of a high-stakes task, MrBeast's films generate powerful emotions that urge viewers to watch to the end. By blending spectacle with emotion, he guarantees his content creates a lasting effect.

3.2 Experimenting with Formats and Ideas

Innovation has always been at the core of MrBeast's content approach. Experimenting with various formats and concepts keeps his channel fresh and entertaining, ensuring that fans never know what to expect next. From presenting intricate challenges to replicating renowned cultural events, Jimmy has perfected the art of renewing his material.

One of MrBeast's most notable assets is his willingness to take chances. He's not hesitant to attempt unique ideas, even if there's no guarantee of success. For instance, his video where he counted to 100,000 may have easily been considered as tedious. Instead, it became a viral hit, showcasing the power of originality.

Collaboration has also played a significant part in his content experimentation. By engaging with other producers and influencers, MrBeast has been able to provide fresh viewpoints and reach new audiences. These partnerships typically result in creative synergies that increase the quality and impact of his videos.

MrBeast's staff is another crucial component in his capacity to explore. Behind the scenes, a committed gang of writers, editors, and producers works diligently to bring his ideas to reality. This collaborative atmosphere stimulates innovation and guarantees that even the most demanding projects are done correctly.

3.3 Learning from Failures

Every great creative recognizes the significance of learning from setbacks, and MrBeast is no different. While his channel is now associated with success, the path has been riddled with hurdles and failures. Early in his career, Jimmy encountered the same problems as many ambitious creators—low view counts, limited resources, and the urge to stand out on a crowded platform.

One of the most essential things MrBeast has learnt is the necessity of persistence. Many of his early videos failed to acquire popularity, but instead of giving up, he embraced these events as chances to learn and develop. By examining what worked and what didn't, he was able to tweak his material and get a greater knowledge of his audience.

Another lesson has been the significance of adaptation. Not every concept turns out as intended, and some initiatives have underperformed despite tremendous effort and expense. Rather of concentrating on these setbacks, MrBeast considers them as experiments that add to his progress. This perspective helps him to approach each new video with newfound passion and a drive to experiment.

Failure has also taught MrBeast the significance of resilience. The pressure to always outdo himself might be overpowering, but Jimmy has learned to enjoy the challenge. By keeping focused on his long-term objectives and having a positive mindset, he has been able to handle setbacks and continue pushing the frontiers of content production.

Mastering the art of content production is a never-ending process, and MrBeast's path provides significant lessons for producers worldwide. Through meticulous preparation, continuous experimentation, and a willingness to learn from errors, Jimmy Donaldson has established a new benchmark for what's possible on YouTube. His ability to mix creativity with strategy has not only garnered him millions of followers but also secured his reputation as one of the most inventive innovators of his generation

.

CHAPTER 4: PHILANTHROPY AND IMPACT

4.1 Giving Back: The Birth of Generous Challenges

Philanthropy has always been at the center of MrBeast's purpose, putting him apart from many other content makers. The thought of giving back came early in his career when he understood the power of his platform to effect significant change. His generous challenges, where people participate in unusual activities to earn life-changing gifts, have become a feature of his channel.

The notion of benevolent challenges was formed out of a simple philosophy: to utilize achievement as a tool for good effect. Whether it's offering cash to strangers, tipping waitstaff with gold bars, or donating homes and automobiles, MrBeast's challenges grab the hearts of millions. These acts of compassion not only aid the beneficiaries but also encourage people worldwide to embrace giving.

One of the most startling characteristics of MrBeast's humanitarian challenges is the magnitude. His willingness to take financial risks, sometimes investing millions in a single video, demonstrates his commitment to creating impactful content. Behind the scenes, meticulous planning and coordination ensure that these challenges are executed seamlessly. From selecting deserving participants to orchestrating complex logistics, every detail is carefully considered.

The ripple effect of these challenges extends beyond the immediate beneficiaries. They highlight the transformative power of kindness and encourage others to think about how they can make a difference in their communities. MrBeast's content proves that generosity can be entertaining, impactful, and deeply rewarding.

4.2 Team Trees and Team Seas: Global Movements

In addition to his individual acts of kindness, MrBeast has spearheaded global movements that address pressing environmental issues. Team Trees, launched in 2019, was a groundbreaking initiative aimed at planting 20 million trees worldwide. Partnering with the Arbor Day Foundation and fellow YouTuber Mark Rober, the campaign raised over $20 million in just a few months.

Team Trees demonstrated the power of collective action. By rallying his audience and leveraging the influence of other creators, MrBeast turned an ambitious idea into a global phenomenon. The campaign's success showcased the potential of social media to drive real-world change and inspired countless other creators to launch philanthropic initiatives.

Building on the success of Team Trees, MrBeast and Mark Rober launched Team Seas in 2021, an initiative to remove 30 million pounds of trash from oceans, rivers, and beaches. Partnering with Ocean Conservancy and The Ocean Cleanup, the campaign raised over $30 million, further solidifying MrBeast's reputation as a leader in environmental advocacy.

Both campaigns highlight MrBeast's ability to mobilize a global audience for a common cause. By using his platform to address critical issues, he has shown that content creators can play a significant role in shaping a better future. Team Trees and Team Seas have left a lasting legacy, proving that even seemingly insurmountable challenges can be tackled through unity and determination.

4.3 Inspiring Others to Make a Difference

One of MrBeast's biggest successes is his ability to inspire people. His humanitarian initiatives have created a surge of giving, pushing people and businesses alike to think imaginatively about how they may give to society. From little acts of kindness to large-scale projects, his impact is visible in the innumerable tales of individuals following in his footsteps.

MrBeast's material serves as a reminder that anybody can make a difference, regardless of their means. His movies generally underscore the value of beginning small and working within one's limits. Whether it's providing time, money, or talents, the message is clear: every effort matters.

Moreover, MrBeast's honesty about his humanitarian endeavors has created a new norm for accountability in philanthropy. By recording the process and results, he guarantees that his audience sees the concrete effect of their support. This openness creates trust and promotes the concept that giving back is not simply an act of charity but also a duty.

The ripple effect of MrBeast's altruism stretches beyond his direct audience. By cooperating with other producers, partnering with non-profits, and connecting with his community, he has established a movement that transcends the digital realm. His work has encouraged a new generation of producers to go beyond entertainment and examine how their platforms may be utilized for good.

Through his charitable challenges, worldwide movements, and attempts to inspire others, MrBeast has revolutionized what it means to be a content producer. His devotion to charity and effect serves as a light of hope, illustrating that success can be a driver for good change. As his influence continues to grow, so does his potential to make an even greater difference in the world

.

CHAPTER 5: THE BUSINESS EMPIRE

5.1 Launching Beast Burger

The launch of MrBeast Burger marked a transformative moment in the content creator's career, demonstrating his ability to translate digital success into a real-world business empire. Introduced in December 2020, Beast Burger redefined the traditional restaurant model by leveraging the growing popularity of virtual kitchens. Unlike conventional brick-and-mortar establishments, MrBeast Burger operates as a delivery-only brand, partnering with existing kitchens to prepare its menu items.

The initial launch was a spectacle in itself, showcasing MrBeast's signature blend of generosity and innovation. To promote the brand, he hosted a grand opening event, giving away free burgers, money, and even a car to unsuspecting customers. This viral marketing strategy not only generated massive media coverage but also set the tone for the brand's identity—a mix of fun, quality, and accessibility. At its core, Beast Burger represents a deep understanding of modern consumer behavior. The menu, designed to appeal to a wide audience, features comfort food classics such as burgers, fries, and chicken sandwiches. By integrating his personal branding into the product names, like the "Beast Style" burger, MrBeast created an immediate connection with his audience.

The rapid expansion of Beast Burger is a testament to its success. Within a year, the brand grew to hundreds of locations across the United

States and internationally. This scalability was made possible by strategic partnerships with virtual kitchen networks, allowing the brand to reach new markets without the overhead costs of traditional restaurant chains.

5.2 Diversifying with Merchandise and Products

Beyond Beast Burger, MrBeast has built a diverse portfolio of merchandise and products that contribute to his business empire. From clothing lines to limited-edition collectibles, his merchandise operations exemplify the power of leveraging a loyal fan base.

The design of MrBeast's merchandise reflects his unique brand identity, featuring bold colors, creative graphics, and playful designs. These items are not just products; they're an extension of his online persona, allowing fans to feel more connected to his world. The inclusion of exclusive drops and limited-edition items creates a sense of urgency, driving demand and fostering a sense of community among buyers.

MrBeast's approach to merchandise goes beyond aesthetics. He prioritizes quality and sustainability, ensuring that his products align with his values. By partnering with ethical manufacturers and exploring eco-friendly materials, he has positioned his merchandise as both desirable and responsible.

In addition to apparel, MrBeast has ventured into other product categories, such as branded snacks and gaming accessories. Each new product launch is strategically timed and promoted, often accompanied by engaging content that showcases the items in action. This cross-promotion not only boosts sales but also reinforces his brand's identity as innovative and forward-thinking.

5.3 Partnerships and Collaborations

Collaboration has been a cornerstone of MrBeast's success, extending beyond his content to his business ventures. By forming strategic partnerships with industry leaders, he has amplified his reach and diversified his revenue streams.

One of the most notable partnerships is his collaboration with Virtual Dining Concepts for Beast Burger. This partnership enabled him to scale his brand rapidly, leveraging the expertise and infrastructure of an established company. Similarly, his partnerships with platforms like Shopify and Teespring have streamlined the logistics of his merchandise operations, allowing him to focus on creativity and growth.

MrBeast's collaborations also extend to other creators and brands. By teaming up with fellow YouTubers, he has co-created products and campaigns that resonate with their shared audiences. These collaborations not only drive sales but also strengthen his relationships within the creator community.

Brand endorsements and sponsorships are another significant aspect of his business empire. However, MrBeast is selective about the brands he associates with, ensuring they align with his values and appeal to his audience. This careful curation has helped him maintain authenticity while maximizing profitability.

Through ventures like Beast Burger, diversified merchandise, and strategic partnerships, MrBeast has established himself as more than just a content creator. His business empire reflects his entrepreneurial spirit, creativity, and commitment to delivering value to his audience. As he continues to innovate and expand, his influence in both the digital and real-world economies is set to grow exponentially.

CHAPTER 6: THE MAN BEHIND THE BRAND

6.1 Balancing Fame and Personal Life

Behind the immense success and global recognition of MrBeast lies a man striving to balance the demands of fame with the realities of personal life. As one of the most prominent figures on YouTube, Jimmy Donaldson—better known as MrBeast—faces the unique challenge of maintaining a sense of normalcy while managing a brand that reaches millions.

Balancing fame and personal life is no small feat, especially when your every move is scrutinized by fans, media, and critics alike. For

Jimmy, this balance begins with setting boundaries. Despite his public persona, he has always been careful to keep certain aspects of his private life out of the spotlight. This separation allows him to preserve his mental health and maintain meaningful relationships away from the camera.

Another key factor in managing fame is time management. With multiple ventures, constant content creation, and a growing business empire, Jimmy's schedule is packed. Yet, he makes a conscious effort to carve out time for himself and his loved ones. Whether it's spending a quiet evening with close friends or taking a break to recharge, these moments are essential for sustaining his energy and focus.

Fame also brings immense pressure to meet expectations, both from fans and from within. Jimmy's commitment to his audience is unwavering, but he has learned the importance of prioritizing his well-being. By delegating tasks, building a reliable team, and leaning on his support system, he ensures that his personal life doesn't take a backseat to his career.

6.2 The Importance of a Support System

No success story is complete without the people who stand behind it, and for Jimmy Donaldson, his support system plays a pivotal role. From family and friends to the dedicated team that helps bring his ideas to life, these individuals form the backbone of his journey.

Jimmy often credits his mother for instilling in him the values of hard work and generosity. Her encouragement and guidance laid the foundation for his success. Similarly, his close circle of friends has been instrumental in providing emotional support and constructive feedback. These relationships are built on trust and mutual respect, allowing Jimmy to navigate the highs and lows of his career with confidence.

One of the most notable aspects of Jimmy's support system is his team. The people who work behind the scenes—editors, producers, coordinators, and more—are crucial to the success of MrBeast's ventures. By surrounding himself with talented and like-minded individuals, Jimmy has created an environment where creativity and collaboration thrive.

The support system extends to his audience as well. Jimmy's fans are not just passive viewers; they are an active and engaged community that fuels his passion. Their unwavering loyalty and enthusiasm motivate him to keep pushing boundaries and delivering content that resonates.

6.3 Staying Humble Amidst Success

Despite his meteoric rise to fame, Jimmy Donaldson remains remarkably grounded. His humility is evident in the way he interacts with fans, collaborates with peers, and approaches his work. This trait has not only endeared him to his audience but also set him apart in an industry often characterized by ego and competition.

One of the key factors contributing to Jimmy's humility is his perspective on success. He views his accomplishments as a result of teamwork, luck, and hard work rather than solely his own efforts. This mindset keeps him grounded and focused on giving back rather than basking in personal glory.

Jimmy's philanthropic efforts also reflect his humility. By prioritizing impact over profit, he demonstrates a commitment to using his platform for good. Whether it's donating to charity, funding environmental initiatives, or helping individuals in need, his actions speak louder than words.

Additionally, Jimmy's willingness to acknowledge his mistakes and learn from them showcases his authenticity. He openly shares his journey, including the challenges and failures, with his audience. This transparency fosters a sense of relatability and reinforces the idea that success is a continuous process of growth and learning.

Through his ability to balance fame and personal life, his reliance on a strong support system, and his commitment to staying humble, Jimmy

Donaldson exemplifies what it means to be a grounded and impactful leader. The man behind the brand is not just a visionary creator but also a testament to the values of resilience, generosity, and authenticity.

CHAPTER 7: CHALLENGES AND CONTROVERSIES

7.1 Overcoming Criticism and Backlash

As one of the most recognizable figures in digital media, Jimmy Donaldson, popularly known as MrBeast, has not been immune to criticism and backlash. While his innovative content and philanthropic endeavors have earned him widespread acclaim, they have also attracted scrutiny and, at times, controversy.

Criticism often arises in response to the scale of Jimmy's projects. Detractors question the motives behind his generosity, accusing him of using philanthropy as a marketing tool. Others critique the spectacle of his giveaways, arguing that they overshadow the causes he aims to support. Jimmy has consistently addressed these criticisms with transparency, emphasizing that his primary goal is to inspire others to do good. He often explains that using his platform to create impactful change is a win-win, benefiting both his audience and the causes he champions.

Backlash has also stemmed from missteps in content execution. As a creator who frequently pushes boundaries, not every project resonates as intended. For example, logistical errors, unforeseen consequences, or cultural misunderstandings have occasionally sparked negative reactions. In such instances, Jimmy's approach has been to acknowledge mistakes openly and take corrective action, demonstrating a willingness to learn and grow.

Jimmy's ability to overcome criticism lies in his resilience and focus on the bigger picture. By staying true to his values and remaining transparent with his audience, he has turned challenges into opportunities for growth. His handling of backlash serves as a reminder that even the most well-intentioned efforts can face hurdles, but perseverance and accountability can pave the way forward.

7.2 Navigating the Pressure of Fame

Fame brings with it a unique set of challenges, and for someone as influential as MrBeast, the pressure can be immense. The constant spotlight, unrelenting expectations, and demands of maintaining a public persona can take a toll on anyone.

One of the most significant pressures Jimmy faces is the need to consistently outdo himself. With each viral video and ambitious project, the bar is set higher, creating a cycle of ever-increasing expectations. This drive for innovation, while fueling his success, also comes with stress and burnout risks. To manage this, Jimmy has built a strong team that shares his vision, allowing him to delegate responsibilities and focus on creativity.

The scrutiny that accompanies fame is another challenge. Every decision Jimmy makes, whether personal or professional, is subject to public opinion. Navigating this scrutiny requires a thick skin and a clear sense of self. Jimmy's strategy involves staying authentic and prioritizing his core values over external validation. By focusing on his mission to entertain and give back, he remains grounded despite the pressures of fame.

Fame also impacts personal relationships. The demands of being a public figure can strain connections with family and friends. Jimmy has addressed this by maintaining a close-knit circle of trusted individuals who understand and support his journey. These relationships provide a sense of normalcy and stability amidst the chaos of his career.

7.3 Lessons Learned from Adversity

Adversity has been a recurring theme in Jimmy Donaldson's journey, shaping him into the resilient and determined individual he is today. Each challenge, whether personal or professional, has provided valuable lessons that continue to guide his path.

One of the most important lessons Jimmy has learned is the value of adaptability. The fast-paced nature of digital media means that trends and audience preferences can change overnight. By staying flexible and open to experimentation, Jimmy has been able to pivot when necessary and maintain his relevance in an ever-evolving landscape.

Another key lesson is the importance of transparency. Whether addressing controversies or sharing his creative process, Jimmy's openness has fostered trust and loyalty among his audience. This transparency extends to acknowledging failures, which he views as opportunities for growth rather than setbacks.

Adversity has also taught Jimmy the significance of mental health. The pressures of his career have underscored the need for self-care and balance. By prioritizing his well-being and seeking support when needed, he has demonstrated that success should not come at the expense of personal happiness.

Finally, adversity has reinforced Jimmy's commitment to his mission. Challenges and controversies have tested his resolve, but they have also deepened his understanding of his purpose. Through perseverance and a focus on the greater good, he has turned obstacles into stepping stones for greater impact.

In navigating criticism, managing the pressures of fame, and learning from adversity, Jimmy Donaldson exemplifies resilience and authenticity. These experiences have not only shaped his career but also enriched his perspective, enabling him to continue inspiring millions around the world.

CHAPTER 8: THE FUTURE OF MRBEAST

8.1 Plans for Expanding the Brand

As one of the most innovative content creators in the digital space, Jimmy Donaldson, better known as MrBeast, shows no signs of slowing down. His vision for the future involves taking the MrBeast brand to unprecedented heights, transforming it into a global empire that extends far beyond YouTube.

One major focus is the expansion of his business ventures. With the success of Beast Burger and his merchandise line, Jimmy has demonstrated a keen ability to identify and capitalize on opportunities. Future plans include scaling these operations, possibly introducing new product lines and international expansions. Beast Burger, for instance, has the potential to become a household name worldwide, rivaling traditional fast-food chains by leveraging its connection to his massive fanbase.

Additionally, Jimmy has hinted at diversifying his content. While his core YouTube channel will remain a priority, he plans to explore new platforms and formats. This includes venturing into long-form storytelling, documentaries, or even scripted series. By staying ahead of trends and embracing emerging technologies such as virtual reality and artificial intelligence, MrBeast aims to redefine digital entertainment.

Collaborations are another key element of his strategy. Jimmy understands the power of partnerships in amplifying his reach and impact.

Whether teaming up with other creators, brands, or nonprofit organizations, these collaborations will likely play a significant role in his brand's growth.

8.2 Continuing the Mission of Generosity

At the heart of everything MrBeast does is his commitment to making a difference. His mission of generosity, which has been a defining feature of his career, will continue to guide his endeavors in the years to come.

Jimmy plans to scale up his philanthropic efforts, taking on larger projects with even greater impact. His Team Trees and Team Seas initiatives demonstrated the potential for global movements to effect change. Future campaigns may tackle pressing issues such as climate change, poverty alleviation, or education. By leveraging his platform, Jimmy hopes to inspire millions to join these efforts, amplifying their collective impact.

Another aspect of his mission involves empowering others to give back. Jimmy's approach to philanthropy is not just about what he can do, but also about encouraging his audience to make a difference in their own communities. Through storytelling and creative challenges, he aims to spark a ripple effect of kindness and generosity.

The integration of charitable elements into his business ventures is also a priority. Whether it's donating a portion of Beast Burger profits to hunger relief or using merchandise sales to fund philanthropic projects, Jimmy's goal is to create a sustainable model where success and social impact go hand in hand.

8.3   Inspiring   the   Next Generation

One of Jimmy Donaldson's greatest legacies may be the inspiration he provides to the next generation of creators and changemakers. Through his journey, he has shown that with creativity, determination, and a willingness to take risks, it's possible to achieve remarkable success while making a positive impact.

Jimmy's mentorship of up-and-coming creators is a testament to his commitment to inspiring others. By sharing insights into his creative process and business strategies, he empowers others to follow in his footsteps. Whether through behind-the-scenes content, workshops, or direct collaborations, Jimmy aims to equip the next wave of talent with the tools they need to succeed.

Education is another area where Jimmy's influence is growing. His focus on innovative and accessible ways to share knowledge, such as creating educational content or funding scholarships, reflects his belief in the power of learning. By investing in education, he hopes to provide opportunities for those who might not otherwise have access to resources that can change their lives.

Looking ahead, Jimmy envisions a world where his work inspires a culture of giving and creativity. His journey serves as a blueprint for how to balance ambition with purpose, encouraging others to think beyond themselves and contribute to a greater good.

With ambitious plans to expand his brand, a steadfast commitment to generosity, and a passion for inspiring the next generation, the future of MrBeast is as bright as ever. Jimmy Donaldson's journey is far from over, and the impact he's poised to make in the years ahead promises to be nothing short of extraordinary.

NOTE

NOTE

NOTE

NOTE

NOTE

NOTE

NOTE